WEIGHT WAT

Freestyle and Flex 2018

Slow Cooker Recipes

Daniel Fisher

Copyright page

ISBN-13: **978-1-948191-35-7**

ISBN-10: 1-948191-35-0

Printed in The U.S.A

Table of Content

Table of Contents

Introduction

I love, love, love the Weight Watchers Freestyle and Flex Plan, don't you? While most weight loss plans say NO! Weight Watchers says **YES!** Yes to all those wonderfully delicious slow cooker comfort foods, like Slow Cooker Beef Stew, Slow Cooker Chili, Slow Cooker Chicken and Dumplings, Slow Cooker Barbecued Ribs, Slow Cooker Beef Stroganoff, Slow Cooker Pot Roast and More!

Wow, it's amazing! With Weight Watchers Freestyle & Flex Slow cooker Recipes, you will be eating such delicious foods, you won't even feel like you're on a diet. I guarantee it! We have done all the work for you with the New Freestyle Smart Points already counted for you, between 1 to 5 Weight Watchers Freestyle Points per serving.

All you have to do is cook and eat! Make **2018 YOUR** year to lose weight and feel great with the help of Weight Watchers. What's new at Weight Watchers? Weight Watchers is now offering New Zero Points Meals you don't have to worry about counting their points!

There are about 200 foods that are zero Points.

This Cookbook features tried and true Slow cooker Recipes for the New Weight Watchers Freestyle and Flex you'll love!

Enjoy!

Weight Watchers Freestyle & Flex Plan

- The weight watchers diet is the best diet, with lots of people recording maximum and healthy weight loss over the years. In light of this, the weight watcher developed a new plan in November 2017.

- The name of the new plan became Flex Plan for the UK Folks and Freestyle Plan for the US, instead of the Previous Plan; Beyond The Scale. Lots of People are already recording healthy weight loss with this Plan for the New Year.

- In the Freestyle Plan, food points are still calculated using the same Measurements of calories, carbohydrates, sugar and fats. Although, this plan incorporate most of the Foods.

- From the Previous plan, Weight watchers has added a whole bunch of new foods you can Freestyle. The Best Part is that, these Meals don't need to be tracked or measured, you can eat the food you love and still lose weight.

Freestyle Zero Point Foods

- The New Weight watchers plan is making losing weight very easy, they have included lots of yummy foods you'll enjoy; this include plant based protein sources like turkey, eggs, tofu, chicken, lentils, yogurt and beans with lean animal inclusive. In addition, you'll get to enjoy your favorite sweetcorn and peas freely on the new plans.

The Zero Point Food The Freestyle Plan

- Boneless skinless turkey breast

- Thin sliced deli chicken breast

- Ground lean chicken

- Fresh, frozen, and canned beans and lentils that are packed without oil or sugar (Lentils, pinto beans, chickpeas, black beans, kidney beans, split peas, soy beans, and more)

- Boneless skinless chicken breast

- Thin sliced deli turkey breast

- Ground lean turkey

- Canned fish that is packed in water or brine (i.e. canned tuna or canned salmon in water)

- All fish and shellfish (this does not include smoked or dried fish)

- Tofu and smoked tofu

- Eggs

- Quorn fillets, ground Quorn, and Quorn pieces (meat substitute)

- Plain soy yogurt

Losing weight on Weight watchers

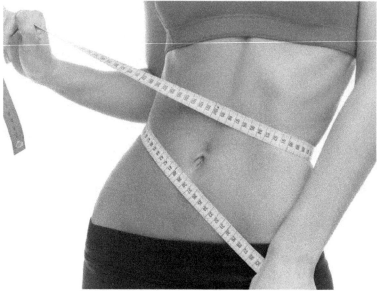

There are two approaches to losing weight on weight watchers

1. Count Smartpoint approach – this allows one to eat whichever food, using the daily and weekly budgets- giving one the

freedom and flexibility of eating whatever they want.

2. No Count Approach/ Freestyle- this allows one a selected list of healthy foods, which should be strictly followed. However, one isn't expected to count or track them – and a weekly allowance for foods not included on the list is given.

In theory, it is believed that about 3500 calories is equivalent to one pound of body weight, and using this as a basis- to lose a pound each week, one must reduce their intake by about 500 calories a day, and by making those changes in one's diet, one can lose an a average of two pounds in a week. Although this value is not uniform in the subsequent weeks on weight watchers- some weeks one might lose more or less than two pounds, one, however can be certain they're on the right tract if one averages the loss of two pounds at the end of the month (4*2/ 2). The weight lost during the first month is usually rapid due to the body's adjustment to the healthier consumption of food. The weight however been lost is known as the water weight, the body fat requires a longer time to be burned off and hence the need for earning fit points.

Weight watchers Tools

- Weight watchers App- this offers personalized benefits, such as food and fitness tracking; a review into one's weight loss journey, a coach, and the most popular feature: Connect community, where one can share their weight loss journey with other members of the community.

- Weight watchers Points tracker – this enables one to keep track of points value as well as monitor one's daily food intake. It allows one save their favorite foods, so they can be tracked easily, allowing one to see their eating history as well as plan ahead.

- Weight Tracker and Progress Charts – members weights are measured weekly, tracks measurement, and progress statistic is plotted.

- Find and Explore – this provides access to over 31,000 food options, with over 1500 recipes to choose from. It also contains suggestions for favorite take out and restaurant meals for the weekends.

- Weight Watchers Points Calculator – this calculate the values in the food.

- Activity Points Calculator - this calculates the number of points a member earns by exercising.

Others includes: Food scale, Measuring cups and spoons, Food Scanner, Body weight scale, Apple watch, Pocket calculator.

N.B some of the tools are more useful to members who decide to stick with the older plan.

Weight Watchers Delicious Slow Cooker Recipes

We have prepared for you in this section, Mouthwatering Weight Watchers Slow Cooker Recipes for the Freestyle and Flex Plan. All the Recipes Comes with Serving Size and Points.

We're not perfect, there might be mistakes with some of the Points, you can also calculate the Smart points value on your own to be double sure. Thanks for believing in us and buying our cookbook. You won't be Disappointed!

WW Freestyle Slow Cooker London Broil

Ingredients:

2 Pound London Broil
1-2 Onions, Sliced
4-6 Garlic Cloves, Minced
4-6 Carrots, Cut Into 1 Inch Pieces
2-4 Celery Ribs, Cut Into 1 Inch Pieces
2 Medium Potatoes, Quartered
1 Can Condensed French Onion Soup

How you make it:

Place the London broil in the bottom of your slow cooker, add the remaining ingredients, cover and cook on low 7-9 hours.

Each 4 Ounce Serving Is 4 Weight Watchers Freestyle Points Servings

Freestyle Slow Cooker Chicken Stroganoff

Ingredients:

1 Pound Chicken Breast Cubes

Salt, Pepper And Garlic Powder To Taste

2 Teaspoons Vegetable Oil

1 Large Sweet Onion, Chopped

3 Cups Chicken Broth

1-3 Teaspoons Worcestershire Sauce

5 Ounces Dry White Wine

2 Bay Leaves

3 Rosemary Sprigs

1-2 Teaspoons Dried Parsley

Salt and Pepper To Taste

2 Pounds Fresh Mushrooms, Sliced

16 Ounces Fat Free Sour Cream

How you make it:

Season the chicken with the salt, pepper and garlic powder. In a large skillet, heat the oil to medium-high. Add the chicken and onions and brown the chicken on all sides; transfer to your slow cooker. Stir in the chicken broth, Worcestershire sauce, burgundy, bay leaves, rosemary, parsley, salt and pepper. Cover and cook on low 6-8 hours. Stir in the mushrooms and sour cream and continue cooking on low 1-2 hours. Remove bay leaves before serving.

Makes Six 3 Weight Watchers Freestyle Point Servings

All New Freestyle Slow Cooker Spanish Bean Soup

Ingredients:

1 Cup Canned Garbanzo Beans
2 Ounces Chorizo Sausage, Sliced
1 Ounce Salt Pork, Cut Into Thin Strips
1 Onion, Finely Chopped
2-4 Garlic Cloves, Minced
2 (5 Inch) Potatoes, Peeled And Cut Into Quarters
1 Ham Bone
1 Beef Bone
6-8 Cups Chicken Broth
Pinch Of Saffron
1 Teaspoon Paprika
Salt And Pepper To Taste

How you make it:

Combine all ingredients in your slow cooker and stir to mix. Cover and cook on low 6-8 hours.

Makes Five 3 Weight Watchers Freestyle Smart Point Servings

WW Flex Cooker Scallops, Zucchini and Tomatoes

Ingredients:

1 Onion, Chopped

3-6 Garlic Cloves, Minced

2 Zucchinis, Diced

28 Ounce Can Diced Tomatoes

2 Tablespoons Tomato Paste

1 Cup Chopped Fresh Basil

Crushed Red Pepper Flakes To Taste

Salt And Pepper To Taste

16 Large Scallops

How you make it:

Combine all ingredients except for the scallops in your slow cooker and stir to mix. Cover and cook on low 5-7 hours, stirring occasionally. Stir in the scallops and continue cooking 1-2 hours.

Makes Eight 1 Weight Watchers Freestyle Points Servings

Freestyle Slow Cooker Jambalaya

Ingredients:
14 Ounces Skinless Chicken Breasts, Cut Into 1 Inch Cubes
2 Ounces Andouille Sausage, Sliced
28 Ounce Can Diced Tomatoes
2 Onions, Chopped
2-4 Garlic Cloves, Minced
1 Green Bell Pepper, Chopped
2 Celery Ribs, Sliced
1 Cup Chicken Broth
2 Teaspoons Dried Oregano
1/2 Teaspoon Dried Thyme
2 Teaspoons Dried Parsley
1 Tablespoon Cajun Seasoning
Cayenne Pepper To Taste
Salt And Pepper To Taste
1 Cup Shrimp, Peeled And De-Veined

How you make it:

Combine all ingredients except for the shrimp in your slow cooker and stir to mix. Cover and cook on low 6-8 hours. Stir in the shrimp and continue cooking another hour until the shrimps are cook through.

Makes Six 3 Weight Watchers Freestyle Points Servings

Freestyle Slow Cooker Honey Lemon Chicken

Ingredients:
8 Skinless Bone-In Chicken Drumsticks
Salt, Pepper, Garlic Powder And Paprika To Taste
1 Tablespoons Vegetable Oil
1 Onion, Chopped
2-4 Garlic Cloves, Minced
1/4 Cup Fresh Lemon Juice Or To Taste
1/2 Cup Honey
1 Teaspoon Thyme
Salt And Pepper To Taste

How you make it:

Season your chicken drumsticks with the salt, pepper, garlic powder and paprika.

In a large skillet heat the oil to medium-high and brown the chicken on all sides; place in the bottom of your slow cooker.

In a medium bowl combine the onion, garlic, lemon juice, honey, thyme, salt and pepper and stir to mix. Pour the mixture over your chicken. Cover and cook on low 6-8 hours.

Each Drumstick Is 3 Weight Watchers Freestyle Points.

Flex On Slow Cooker Crab Stew

Ingredients:

28 Ounce Can Of Stewed Tomatoes
32 Ounces Beef Stock
1 Large Onion, Chopped
2-4 Garlic Cloves, Minced
3 Carrots, Sliced
2 Celery Ribs, Sliced
1 Cup Lima Beans
1 Cup Corn Kernels
2 Tablespoons Old Bay Seasoning
Salt And Pepper To Taste
2 Cups Lump Crab Meat

How you make it:

Combine the tomatoes, beef stock, onion, garlic, carrots, celery, lima beans, corn, Old Bay, salt and pepper in your slow cooker and stir to mix. Cover and cook on low 5-7 hours, stirring occasionally. Add the crab and continue to cook another hour or until the crab is cooked.

Makes Twelve 1 Weight Watchers Freestyle Smart Points Servings

Flex Slow Cooker Chicken Marsala

Ingredients

21 Ounces Skinless Chicken Breasts
Salt, Pepper And Garlic Powder To Taste
1 Tablespoons Vegetable Oil
2 Sweet Onions, Sliced
2-4 Garlic Cloves, Minced
2 Pounds Fresh Mushrooms, Sliced
1/2 Cup Chicken Broth
1 Cup Marsala Wine
Salt And Pepper To Taste

How you make it:

Season your chicken breasts with the salt, pepper and garlic on both sides.

In a large skillet heat the oil to medium-high and brown the chicken on both sides; transfer to your slow cooker.

Add the onion, garlic and mushrooms.

Pour the chicken broth and wine all over and sprinkle with the salt and pepper.

Cover and cook on low 6-8 hours.

Makes Eight Servings

Weight Watcher Smart Points: 1

Freestyle Slow Cooker Award Winning Chili

Ingredients:

12 Ounces Ground Sirloin
1 Large Onion, Roughly Chopped
3-6 Garlic Cloves, Minced
Salt, Pepper And Garlic Powder To Taste
1 Red Bell Pepper, Roughly Chopped
1 Green Bell Pepper, Roughly Chopped
28 Ounce Can Of Whole Tomatoes
28 Ounce Can Of Crushed Tomatoes
1 Cup Canned Dark Red Kidney Beans
1 Cup Canned Light Red Kidney Beans
1 Tablespoon Sugar
1/4 Cup Apple Cider Vinegar
1 Teaspoon Paprika Or To Taste
2 Teaspoons Cumin
1 Teaspoon Basil
1 Tablespoon Chili Powder
Red Pepper Flakes To Taste
Hot Sauce To Taste
Salt And Pepper To Taste

How you make it:

In a large skillet, combine the ground sirloin, onion and garlic; sprinkle with the salt, pepper and garlic powder.

Heat to medium high and brown the beef, stirring occasionally. Transfer the mixture to your slow cooker.

Stir in the remaining ingredients.
Cover and cook on low 8-10 hours, stirring occasionally.

Makes Five Servings

Weight Watchers Freestyle Smart point: 4

Freestyle Slow Cooker BBQ Pulled Pork

Ingredients:
2 Onions, Sliced
2 Garlic Cloves, Minced
1 Pound Lean Pork Butt
Salt, Pepper And Garlic Powder To Taste
Liquid Smoke To Taste
1 Cup Barbecue Sauce

How you make it:
Place the onions and garlic cloves in the bottom of your slow cooker. Season the pork with the salt, pepper and garlic; place on top of the onions and garlic. Pour the liquid smoke and barbecue sauce all over. Cover and cook on low 6-8 hours. Remove to pull the pork and return to your slow cooker.

Makes Seven Servings

Weight Watchers Freestyle Smart Points : 4

Freestyle Slow Cooker BBQ Ribs

Ingredients:

2 Onions, Sliced
4-6 Whole Garlic Cloves
2 Pounds Pork Baby Back Ribs, Fat Removed
1 Tablespoon Chili Powder
1 Teaspoon Thyme
Salt And Pepper To Taste
1 Cup Barbecue Sauce

How you make it:

Place the onions and garlic in the bottom of your slow cooker.

Season your ribs with the chili powder, thyme, salt and pepper; place over the onions and garlic.

Pour the barbecue sauce all over.

Cover and cook on low 8-10 hours.

Each 3 Ounce Serving

Weight Watchers Freestyle Smart points : 4

Freestyle Slow Cooker Beef Burgundy

Ingredients:
1 Pound Lean Stew Beef, Cubed
2 Tablespoons Flour
Salt, Pepper, Garlic Powder And Onion Powder
To Taste
1 Tablespoon Vegetable Oil
2 Large Onions, Chopped
2-4 Garlic Cloves, Chopped
2 Pounds Fresh Mushrooms, Sliced
2 Cups Beef Broth
1/2 Cup Burgundy
2 Bay Leaves
3 Sprigs Fresh Rosemary
1 Tablespoon Fresh Parsley

How you make it:

Place the stew beef in a Ziploc bag. Add the flour, salt, pepper, garlic powder and onion powder and shake to coat.

Heat the oil to medium-high in a large skillet. Add the beef cubes and brown on all sides; transfer to your slow cooker.

Stir in the remaining ingredients and stir to combine. Cover and cook on low 8-10 hours.

Makes Six Servings

Weight Watchers Freestyle Smart Points : 4

Freestyle Slow Cooker Beef Italiano

Ingredients

1 Pound Lean Beef Roast

Salt, Pepper And Garlic Powder To Taste

2 Sweet Onions, Sliced

4 Garlic Cloves, Minced

1 Green Bell Pepper, Roughly Chopped

1 Red Bell Pepper, Roughly Chopped

28 Ounce Can Of Whole Tomatoes

1 Cup Ragu Spaghetti Sauce

1/2 Cup Burgundy

Italian Seasonings To Taste

Salt and Pepper To Taste

How you make it:

Season your roast with the salt, pepper and garlic powder; place in the bottom of your slow cooker.

Top with the onions, garlic and bell peppers. Pour in the tomatoes, Ragu and burgundy; sprinkle with the Italian seasonings, salt and pepper.

Cover and cook on low 6-8 hours.

Makes Six Servings

Weight Watchers Freestyle Smart points: 5

Freestyle Slow Cooker Beef Stroganoff

Ingredients:

1 Pound Lean Stew Beef, Cubed
Salt, Pepper And Garlic Powder To Taste
2 Teaspoons Vegetable Oil
1 Large Sweet Onion, Chopped
3 Cups Beef Broth
1-3 Teaspoons Worcestershire Sauce
1/4 Cup Burgundy
2 Bay Leaves
3 Rosemary Sprigs
1-2 Teaspoons Dried Parsley
Salt and Pepper To Taste
2 Pounds Fresh Mushrooms, Sliced
16 Ounces Fat Free Sour Cream

How you make it:
Season the lean stew beef with the salt, pepper and garlic powder.

In a large skillet, heat the oil to medium-high. Add the beef and onions and brown the beef

on all sides; transfer
to your slow cooker.

Stir in the beef broth, Worcestershire sauce, burgundy, bay leaves, rosemary, parsley, salt and pepper.

Cover and cook on low 6-8 hours. Stir in the mushrooms and sour cream and continue cooking on low 1-2 hours.

Remove bay leaves before serving.

Makes Six Servings

Weight Watchers Freestyle Smart Points: 3

Freestyle Slow Cooker Beefy Cabbage Stew

Ingredients:

1 Teaspoon Vegetable Oil

1 Pound Lean Stew Beef, Cut Into 1 Inch Pieces

2 Cup Beef Broth

1-2 Onions, Chopped

2-4 Garlic Cloves, Minced

1 Bay Leaf

1 (5 Inch) Potato, Peeled And Cubed

2 Celery Ribs, Sliced

4 Cups Cabbage, Chopped

4 Carrots, Sliced

8 Ounce Can Tomato Sauce

2 Tablespoons Tomato Paste

Salt And Pepper To Taste

How you make it:

In a large skillet heat the oil to medium high and brown your beef on all sides; transfer to your slow cooker.

Stir in the beef broth, onions, garlic and bay leaf.

Cover and cook on low 5-7 hours until the beef is tender.

Stir in the remaining ingredients and continue cooking on low another 2-4 hours until the vegetables are tender.

Remove bay leaf before serving.

Makes Five Servings

Weight Watchers Freestyle Smart Points: 3

Freestyle Slow Cooker Beefy Mushroom Stew

Ingredients:

1 Pound Stew Beef, Cut Into 1 Inch Cubes
2 Tablespoons Flour
1 Tablespoon Vegetable Oil
3 Cups Water
1 Packet McCormick Beef Stew Seasoning Mix
5 Cups Portabella Mushrooms, Thickly Sliced
5 Cups Zero Points Plus Cut-Up Fresh
Vegetables, Such As, Carrots, Onions And
Celery

How you make it:

Place the stew beef and flour in a Ziploc bag
and shake to coat.

Heat the oil in a large skillet to medium-high
and brown your beef cubes on all sides; transfer
to your slow cooker.

Stir in the water and seasoning mix.

Cover and cook on low 6-8 hours until the beef is tender. Stir in the remaining ingredients and continue cooking on low 2-3 hours until the vegetables are tender.

Makes Six Servings

Weight Watchers Freestyle Smart Points: 2

Freestyle Slow Cooker Black Beans and Ham
Ingredients:

1 Pound Dried Black Beans, Soaked Overnight
And Drained
32 Ounces Chicken Broth
1 Tablespoon Vinegar
2 Onions, Chopped
3 Garlic Cloves, Minced
1 Green Pepper, Chopped
1 Ounce Salt Pork, Chopped
6 Ounces Lean Ham, Chopped
1 Teaspoon Paprika
1 Teaspoon Cumin
Salt And Pepper To Taste

How you make it:
Combine all ingredients in your slow cooker
and stir to mix. Cover and cook on low 9-12
hours until the beans are tender.

Each 1/2 Cup Serving Is One Weight Watchers
Freestyle Smart Points

Freestyle Slow Cooker Black-Eyed Peas

Ingredients:

1 Pound Dried Black-Eyed Peas, Soaked
Overnight And Drained
1 Onion, Diced
2 Cloves Garlic, Minced
1 Red Bell Pepper, Diced
1 Jalapeno Pepper, De-Seeded And Minced
6 Ounces Lean Ham, Minced
1 Slice Bacon, Chopped
Cayenne Pepper To Taste
1 Teaspoons Cumin
Salt And Pepper To Taste

How you make it:

Combine all ingredients in your slow cooker
and stir to mix.

Cover and cook on low 9-12 hours until the
beans are tender.

Each 1/2 Cup Serving Is 2 Weight Watchers
Freestyle Smart Points

Freestyle Slow Cooker Chicken and Broccoli

Ingredients:

2 Onions, Sliced
4 Garlic Cloves
24 Ounces Boneless Chicken Breasts
Salt, Pepper, Garlic Powder And Paprika To Taste
6 Cups Broccoli Florets
1 Cup Chicken Broth
Salt, Pepper And Garlic To Taste

How you make it:

Place the onions and garlic in the bottom of your slow cooker.

Season your chicken breasts on each side with the salt, pepper, garlic powder and paprika; arrange on top of your onions and garlic.

Arrange the broccoli on top of the chicken, pour the chicken broth all over and sprinkle with the salt, pepper and garlic.

Cover and cook on low 6-8 hours until the chicken is tender.

Makes Six Servings

Weight Watchers Freestyle Smart Points: 1

Freestyle Slow Cooker Chicken and Fruits

Ingredients:

24 Ounces Skinless Chicken Breasts

1 Mango, Peeled And Sliced

1 Orange; Peeled, De-Seeded And Sliced

1 Pear, Peeled, De-Seeded And Sliced

6 Fresh Pineapple Slices

1-2 Teaspoons Cinnamon

Salt To Taste

How you make it:

Place your chicken breasts in the bottom of your slow cooker. Top with your fruits and sprinkle with the cinnamon and salt. Cover and cook on low 5-7 hours until the chicken is tender.

Makes Six Servings

Weight Watchers Freestyle Smart Points: 1

Freestyle Slow Cooker Chicken and Mushroom Stew

Ingredients:

27 Ounces Skinless Chicken Breasts, Cut Into 1 Inch Cubes
Salt, Pepper And Garlic Powder To Taste
1 Tablespoon Vegetable Oil
1 Medium Onion, Diced
4-6 Garlic Cloves, Minced
1 Green Bell Pepper, Roughly Chopped
1 Cup Fat Free Sun-Dried Tomatoes, Chopped
1 Pound Fresh Mushrooms, Sliced
4 Zucchini, Thickly Sliced
6 Ounce Can Tomato Paste
2 Cups Chicken Broth
Italian Seasonings To Taste
Salt And Pepper To Taste

How you make it:

Season your chicken cubes with the salt, pepper and garlic powder.

In a large skillet heat the oil to medium-high and brown your chicken on all sides; transfer to your slow cooker.

Stir in the remaining ingredients. Cover and cook on low 6-8 hours.

Makes Six Servings

Weight Watchers Freestyle Smart Points : 2

Freestyle Slow Cooker Chicken and Stuffing

Ingredients:

20 Ounces Skinless Chicken Breasts
Salt, Pepper And Garlic Powder To Taste
1 Cup Cream Of Mushroom Soup
1 Cup Chicken Broth
2 Cups Pepperidge Farm Herb Stuffing Mix
2 Teaspoons Poultry Seasoning
1 Sweet Onion, Diced
1-2 Garlic Cloves, Minced
1-2 Celery Ribs, Diced
1 Tablespoon Butter, Melted
Salt And Pepper To Taste

How you make it:
Season your chicken breasts with the salt, pepper and garlic powder; transfer to the bottom of your slow cooker.

In a large bowl, combine the remaining ingredients and mix well.

Place your stuffing mixture on top of your chicken breasts and smooth with a spoon.

Cover and cook on low for 6-8 hours.
Makes Eight Servings

Weight Watchers Freestyle Smart Points: 2

Flex Slow Cooker Chicken Creole

Ingredients

24 Ounces Skinless Chicken Breasts
Salt, Pepper And Creole Seasoning To Taste
28 Ounce Can Stewed Tomatoes
2 Large Onions, Chopped
2-4 Garlic Cloves, Minced
2 Celery Ribs, Diced
1 Green Bell Pepper, Diced
16 Ounces Fresh Mushrooms, Sliced
1 Jalapeno Pepper, De- Seeded And Chopped
Hot Sauce To Taste
Salt And Pepper To Taste
Salt, Pepper And Creole Seasoning To Taste

How you make it:

Season your chicken breasts with the salt, pepper and Creole seasoning on both sides.

Stir in the remaining ingredients.

Cover and cook on low 6-8 hours.

Makes Six Servings

Weight Watchers Freestyle Smart Points: 1

Freestyle Slow Cooker Chicken Marrakesh

Ingredients

24 Ounces Skinless Chicken Breasts
Salt, Pepper And Garlic Powder To Taste
2 Sweet Onions, Sliced
2-4 Garlic Cloves, Minced
2-3 Carrots, Peeled And Diced
1 Large Sweet Potato, Peeled And Diced
28 Ounce Can Diced Tomatoes
3/4 Cup Canned Garbanzo Beans, Drained
1/2 Teaspoon Each Ground Cumin, Turmeric
And Cinnamon
1 Teaspoon Dried Parsley
Salt And Pepper To Taste

How you make it:
Season your chicken breasts with the salt, pepper and garlic; place in the bottom of your slow cooker.

Add the onions, garlic, carrots, sweet potato, tomatoes and garbanzo beans.

Sprinkle with the cumin, turmeric, cinnamon, parsley, salt and pepper.

Cover and cook on low 6-8 hours.

Makes Eight Servings

Weight Watcher Freestyle Smart Points: 2

Flex Slow Cooker Cioppino

Ingredients:

28 Ounce Can Crushed Tomatoes

8 Ounce Can Tomato Sauce

2 Onions, Chopped

2-4 Garlic Cloves, Minced

1 Green Bell Pepper, Chopped

1 Red Bell Pepper, Chopped

1/2 Cup Dry White Wine

2 Teaspoons Olive Oil

1/2 Cup Parsley, Chopped

1 Teaspoon Thyme

2 Teaspoons Basil

1 Teaspoon Oregano

1/2 Teaspoon Paprika

Cayenne Pepper To Taste

Salt And Pepper To Taste

6 Ounces Sea Bass, Snapper Or Grouper

6 Large Shrimp, Peeled And De-Veined

10 Small Scallops

10 Mussels, De-Bearded And Scrubbed

10 Clams, Scrubbed

Lemon Slices For Garnish

How you make it:

Combine the tomatoes, tomato sauce, onions, garlic, bell peppers, wine, olive oil, parsley, thyme, basil, oregano, paprika, cayenne pepper, salt and pepper in your slow cooker and stir to mix.

Cover and cook 6 to 8 hours on low.

Turn your slow cooker on high, add seafood and cook about an hour until the seafood is cooked and the clams have opened.
Discard any clams that haven't opened.

Makes Six Servings

Weight Watcher Freestyle Smart Points: 4

Flex Slow Cooker Corned Beef and Cabbage

Ingredients:

3-4 Pound Corned Beef Brisket With Spice
Packet
2 Onions, Thickly Sliced
2-4 Garlic Cloves, Whole
4 Celery Ribs, Halved
6 Carrots, Roughly Chopped
Chicken Broth
1 Cabbage, Cut Into Large Wedges
Salt And Pepper To Taste

How you make it:

Trim the fat from your corned beef, rinse and
set aside. Place the onions, garlic, celery and
carrots in the bottom of your slow cooker.

Place your corned beef on top of your
vegetables.

Pour enough chicken broth to cover and
sprinkle with your spice packet.

Cover and cook on low for 6-8 hours.

Add the cabbage, salt and pepper and continue cooking another 2-3 hours until the brisket is very tender.

Slice the brisket across the grain to serve.

Each 2 Ounce Slice Of Corned Beef Is 2 Weight Watchers Freestyle Smart Points, The Vegetables Are 0 Weight Watchers Freestyle Smart Points.

Freestyle Slow Cooker Cranberry Pork

Ingredients:

1 Sweet Onion, Sliced
4 Garlic Cloves, Minced
2 Pound Boneless Pork Loin Roast
1 Package Fresh Cranberries
2 Apples; Cored, Peeled And Coarsely Chopped
Liquid Artificial Sweetener To Taste
Salt And Pepper To Taste

How you make it:

Place the sweet onion slices in the bottom of your slow cooker. Rub your pork roast all over with the garlic, place on top of your onion slices. In a large bowl, mix the cranberries, apples, sweetener, salt and pepper together and pour over your pork roast. Cover and cook on low 6-8 hours.

Each 2 Ounce Slice Of Pork Loin Is 3 Weight Watchers Freestyle Servings, The Fruits Are Zero Points

Freestyle Slow Cooker Fish and Vegetables

Ingredients:

18 Ounces Flounder Fillets, Cubed
1 Onion, Sliced
2-4 Garlic Cloves, Minced
1 Green Bell Pepper, Sliced
1 Red Bell Pepper, Sliced
2 Zucchini, Sliced
28 Ounce Can Diced Tomatoes
Basil And Oregano To Taste
Salt And Pepper To Taste

How you make it:
Combine all ingredients in your slow cooker and stir gently. Cover and cook on low 6-8 hours.

Makes Six 2 Weight Watchers Freestyle Servings

Freestyle Slow Cooker Herbed Turkey Breast

Ingredients:
3 Garlic Cloves, Chopped
1 Sweet Onion, Sliced
2 Pounds Skinless Turkey Breast
Salt and Pepper To Taste
3 Sprigs fresh Rosemary
Thyme And Sage To Taste
1/2 Cup Chicken Broth

How you make it:

Place the garlic and onions in the bottom of your crock pot. Place the turkey breast on top of the onions and garlic, sprinkle with salt, pepper, rosemary, thyme and sage. Add the chicken broth, cover and cook on low 6-8 hours.

Each 2 Ounce Serving Is 2 Weight Watchers Freestyle Points Servings

Freestyle Slow Cooker Italian Chicken

Ingredients:
2 Onions, Sliced
2-4 Whole Garlic Cloves
24 Ounces Skinless Chicken Breasts
16 Ounces Fresh Mushrooms, Sliced
1 Green Bell Pepper, Sliced (Optional)
28 Ounce Can Stewed Tomatoes
6 Ounce Can Tomato Paste
1 Package McCormick Slow Cookers Italian
Herb Chicken Seasoning

How you make it:

Place the onions and garlic in the bottom of
your slow cooker.

Arrange the chicken breasts on top of the
onions and garlic; top with the mushrooms and
bell pepper.

In a large bowl combine the tomatoes, tomato paste and seasoning.

Mix well and pour into your slow cooker.

Cover and cook on low 6-8 hours.

Makes Six 3 Weight Watcher Freestyle Points Servings

WW Flex Slow Cooker Rosemary Chicken and Vegetables

Ingredients:

24 Ounces Skinless Chicken Breasts

Salt, Pepper, Rosemary And Garlic To Taste

2 Onions, Chopped

2-4 Garlic Cloves, Minced

1 Jar Fat Free Artichoke Hearts, Drained

4 Carrots, Sliced

4 Celery Ribs, Sliced

1 Tablespoon Rosemary Or To Taste

Salt And Pepper To Taste

How you make it:

Season the chicken breasts with the salt, pepper, rosemary and garlic on both side; place in the bottom of your slow cooker.

Add the onions, garlic, artichoke hearts, carrots and celery.

Sprinkle with the rosemary, salt and pepper. Cover and cook on low 6-8 hours.

Makes Eight 3 Weight Watchers Freestyle Points Servings

WW Freestyle Slow Cooker Savory Beef Stew

Ingredients:

1 Pound Lean Stew Beef, Cubed

2 Tablespoons Flour

1 Tablespoon Vegetable Oil

32 Ounces Beef Broth

1 Package McCormick Beef Stew Mix

1-2 Sweet Onions, Roughly Chopped

3-4 Carrots, Sliced

3-4 Celery Ribs, Sliced

1 (5 Inch) Potato, Peeled and Cubes

How you make it:

Place the stew beef and flour in a large Ziploc bag and shake to coat.

In a large skillet heat the oil to medium-high and brown the beef cubes on all sides; transfer to your slow cooker.

Stir in the beef broth and beef stew mix.

Cover and cook on low 5-7 hours. Stir in the onions, carrots, celery and potatoes; cover and continue cooking on low 2-3 hours.

Makes Six 5 Weight Watchers Freestyle Point Servings

WW Flex Slow Cooker Shrimp Gumbo

Ingredients:

2 Cups Chicken Broth
28 Ounce Can Diced Tomatoes
2 Onions, Diced
1 Green Bell Pepper, Diced
1 Red Bell Pepper, Diced
2 Celery Ribs, Chopped
2 Carrot, Chopped
2 Ounces Polish Sausage, Thickly Sliced6
Dried Oregano And Thyme To Taste
Red Pepper Flakes To Taste
Salt And Pepper To Taste
2 Cups Large Shrimp, Peeled And De-Veined8

How you make it:

Combine all ingredients except for the shrimp in your slow cooker and stir to mix.

Cover and cook on low 6-8 hours. Stir in the shrimp and continue to cook another hour.

Makes Seven 2 Weight Watchers Freestyle Points Servings

Freestyle Slow Cooker Smoked Turkey Legs
Ingredients:

3-4 Turkey Legs
1 Onion, Grated
4 -6 Garlic Cloves, Minced
1/4 Cup Liquid Smoke
Salt And Pepper To Taste
2 Tablespoons Vegetable Oil

How You Make it:

Place the turkey legs in a large Ziploc bag. Add
the onion, garlic, liquid smoke, salt and pepper
and shake to coat. Close the bag and
refrigerate overnight, turning occasionally.
Heat the oil in a large skillet to medium-high
and brown the turkey legs on all sides. Place
the turkey legs in your slow cooker. Cover and
cook on low 8-10 hours.

Each 2 Ounce Serving Is 2 Weight Watchers
Freestyle Points

Flex On Slow Cooker Veggie Chili

Ingredients:
1 Large Onion, Roughly Chopped
3-6 Garlic Cloves, Minced
Salt, Pepper And Garlic Powder To Taste
1 Red Bell Pepper, Roughly Chopped
1 Green Bell Pepper, Roughly Chopped
1 Yellow Bell Pepper, Roughly Chopped
2 Carrots, Chopped
2 Celery Ribs, Chopped
28 Ounce Can Of Whole Tomatoes
28 Ounce Can Of Crushed Tomatoes
1 Cup Canned Dark Red Kidney Beans
1 Cup Canned Light Red Kidney Beans
1 Tablespoon Sugar
1/4 Cup Apple Cider Vinegar
1 Teaspoon Paprika Or To Taste
2 Teaspoons Cumin
1 Teaspoon Basil
1 Tablespoon Chili Powder
Red Pepper Flakes To Taste
Hot Sauce To Taste
Salt And Pepper To Taste

How you make it:

In a large skillet, combine the ground sirloin, onion and garlic; sprinkle with the salt, pepper and garlic powder. Heat to medium high and brown the beef, stirring occasionally. Transfer the mixture to your slow cooker. Stir in the remaining ingredients.

Cover and cook on low 8-10 hours, stirring occasionally.

Makes Six 1 Weight Watchers Flex Points Serving

WW Flex Slow Cooker Chicken Noodle Soup

Ingredients:

1 Pound Chicken Breast, Cut Into 1 Inch Pieces
4 Teaspoons Butter
1-2 Onions, Chopped
4-6 Garlic Cloves, Minced
4-6 Carrots, Cut Into 1 Inch Pieces
2-4 Celery Ribs, Cut Into 1 Inch Pieces
2 Quarts Chicken Broth
Thyme Or Basil To Taste
1-2 Bay Leaves
Salt And Pepper To Taste
2 Cups Cooked Noodles

How you make it:

Combine all ingredients except for the noodles in your slow cooker. Cover and cook on low for 7-9 hours. Add the noodles and heat through.

Makes Ten 3 Weight Watchers Freestyle Smart Points Servings

WW Freestyle Slow Cooker Maple Ham

Ingredients:

1 Bone-In Ham That Fits In Your Slow Cooker
1 Cup Maple Syrup
1/2 Cup Brown Sugar
Ground Cinnamon To Taste
Ground Cloves To Taste

How you make it:

Place the ham in your slow cooker. Whisk together the remaining ingredients and brush over the ham. Cover and cook on low 7-9 hours.

Each 3 Ounce Serving Is 3 Weight Watchers Freestyle Points Servings

Freestyle Slow Cooker Greek Chicken

Ingredients:

25 Ounces Skinless Chicken Breasts
Salt, Pepper And Garlic Powder To Taste
2 Onions, Chopped
3-6 Cloves Garlic, Minced
12 Large Kalamata Olives, Pitted And Chopped
1/2 Cup Fat Free Sun-Dried Tomatoes, Roughly Chopped
1/4 Cup Freshly Squeezed Lemon Juice
1 Tablespoon Balsamic Vinegar
Salt And Pepper To Taste
1/4 Cup Feta Cheese, Crumbled
1/4 Cup Capers
Chopped Fresh Basil

How you make it:
Season your chicken breasts with the salt pepper and garlic on both sides, place in the bottom of your slow cooker.

Add the onions, garlic, olives and tomatoes. Pour the lemon juice and vinegar all over and sprinkle with the salt and pepper.

Cover and cook on low 6-8 hours. Transfer to your serving platter and top with the feta cheese, capers and basil.

Makes Six 5 Weight Watchers Freestyle Servings

Weekly Meal Planner

Weekly Menu Planner

■ Shopping List

Monday

Tuesday

Wednesday

Thursday

Friday

Saturday

Sunday

Conclusion

This Weight Watcher Slow cooker for the New

Plans will help Jumpstart your Weight Loss Goal

Easy and Effortlessly. Lose Weight while Eating

the food you love.

Thank You

Thanks So Much For The Support. If you enjoyed this My Weight Watcher Freestyle & Flex Slow cooker Recipes Take a Little Time to Leave Us A Review.

It will be well appreciated! One or Two Statement Will Go a Long Way in Helping Other People Looking to Buy.

Don't Forget to visit my profile on amazon to get more amazing cookbooks and Journals

Recommendations

Visit this links below to get one Now

Weight Watchers Freestyle 2018 CookBook>> Amazon Link>> http://amzn.to/2Dy0kTm

My Weight Watchers Freestyle Journal 2018>> Amazon link>>
https://www.amazon.com/dp/1948191172

My Weight Watchers Flex Journal 2018 >> Amazon Link>>

https://www.amazon.com/dp/1948191180

My Weight Watchers Freestyle & Flex Instant Pot Recipes>> Amazon Link>>
https://www.amazon.com/dp/1948191199

CPSIA information can be obtained
at www.ICGtesting.com
Printed in the USA
LVHW04s1825250418
574835LV00017B/1090/P

9 781948 191357